IT'S TIME TO EAT GOOSEBERRIES

It's Time to Eat GOOSEBERRIES

Walter the Educator

Silent King Books
A WhichHead Entertainment Imprint

Copyright © 2024 by Walter the Educator

All rights reserved. No part of this book may be reproduced in any manner whatsoever without written per- mission except in the case of brief quotations embodied in critical articles and reviews.

First Printing, 2024

Disclaimer

This book is a literary work; the story is not about specific persons, locations, situations, and/or circumstances unless mentioned in a historical context. Any resemblance to real persons, locations, situations, and/or circumstances is coincidental. This book is for entertainment and informational purposes only. The author and publisher offer this information without warranties expressed or implied. No matter the grounds, neither the author nor the publisher will be accountable for any losses, injuries, or other damages caused by the reader's use of this book. The use of this book acknowledges an understanding and acceptance of this disclaimer.

It's Time to Eat GOOSEBERRIES is a collectible early learning book by Walter the Educator suitable for all ages belonging to Walter the Educator's Time to Eat Book Series. Collect more books at WaltertheEducator.com

USE THE EXTRA SPACE TO TAKE NOTES AND DOCUMENT YOUR MEMORIES

GOOSEBERRIES

Come gather 'round, it's time to see,

It's Time to Eat
Gooseberries

A special fruit, the gooseberry!

Tiny and round, they grow so small,

But they're the yummiest fruit of all!

Green and golden, or even red,

Gooseberries shine in their garden bed.

Smooth and tart, or sweet and bright,

They're a treat for morning, noon, or night!

Pick them gently, don't rush or tug,

They sit on branches, snug as a bug.

Careful now, they're soft and sweet,

A juicy snack that's hard to beat!

Pop one in, feel the juicy flow,

Gooseberries make your smile glow!

A little tart, but that's okay,

Their zingy flavor brightens your day.

It's Time to Eat
Gooseberries

Eat them plain or bake a pie,

Gooseberries make your spirits fly.

Jams and jellies, sauces too,

This tiny fruit has much to do!

Full of goodness, fresh and fun,

They're packed with vitamins for everyone.

Strong and healthy you'll surely be,

With gooseberries, just wait and see!

From garden beds to sunny skies,

Gooseberries are nature's prize.

A berry treat, so pure and true,

A gift from the earth, just for you!

Tart and tangy, sweet and mild,

Gooseberries make every child smile.

Round and tiny, but oh so grand,

It's Time to Eat
Gooseberries

The perfect fruit, right in your hand.

Let's eat them now, don't wait too long,

Gooseberries sing their fruity song!

A snack to share, so fresh and bright,

Gooseberries make the world feel right.

One for you and one for me,

Let's have a gooseberry jubilee!

It's gooseberry time, so don't be late,

It's Time to Eat
Gooseberries

A fruity feast that's truly great!

ABOUT THE CREATOR

Walter the Educator is one of the pseudonyms for Walter Anderson. Formally educated in Chemistry, Business, and Education, he is an educator, an author, a diverse entrepreneur, and he is the son of a disabled war veteran. "Walter the Educator" shares his time between educating and creating. He holds interests and owns several creative projects that entertain, enlighten, enhance, and educate, hoping to inspire and motivate you. Follow, find new works, and stay up to date with Walter the Educator™ at WaltertheEducator.com

www.ingramcontent.com/pod-product-compliance
Lightning Source LLC
LaVergne TN
LVHW012052070526
838201LV00082B/3990